WOMEN MENTORING WOMEN

Devotional Book #2

Terri Jenkin

"Teach what accords with sound doctrine. . .

Teach what is good."

Titus 2:1, 3

Table of Content

For consistency, all Scripture is taken from the King James Version of the Bible

Introduction:

It is the Word of God that changes lives. My greatest joy and privilege is to teach, challenge and encourage ladies from the Word of God intertwined with experiences in my own life.

I trust these devotionals will help to strengthen your faith as well as encourage you to grow in your knowledge of God.

Terri Jenkin

"I am crucified with Christ: nevertheless I live; yet not I, but Christ liveth in me; and the life which now live in the flesh I live by the faith of the son of God, who love me and gave himself for me."

Galatians 2:20

And the Truth is?

We are often told there is no absolute truth. Yet this is contrary to the very definition of truth: *"that which is* absolutely *reliable, constant, never changing."*

The truth is:
Jesus Christ. *"Jesus saith unto him, 'I am the way, the truth, and the life':"* (John 14:6).

The Gospel. *"In whom ye also trusted, after that ye heard the word of truth, the gospel of your salvation:"* (Ephesians 1:13).

The Word of God. *"Sanctify them through thy truth: thy word is truth"* (John 17:17). *"If ye continue in my word...ye are my disciples indeed; ...ye shall know the truth, and the truth shall make you free"* (John 8:31-32).

The Holy Spirit. *"Howbeit when he, the Spirit of truth, is come, he will guide you into all truth"* (John 16:13).

Only this truth will make a difference in our life:
Our Salvation. *". . .no man cometh unto the Father, but by me"* (John 14:6).

Our Thinking. *"Finally, brethren, whatsoever things are* **true**, . . .think on these things"* (Philippians 4:8).

Our Choices. God wants us to make choices based on the truth of His Word and not on feelings, circumstances or pressures from the outside. *"Study to shew thyself approved unto God, a workman that needeth not to be ashamed, rightly dividing the word of truth"* (2 Timothy 2:15). It is essential that we search God's Word and think biblically so we will evaluate our thoughts, considerations, and decisions against the truth of God's Word.

Our Response to Difficulties. *"Nay, in all these things we are more than conquerors..."* (Romans 8:37).

Our View of Eternity. *"In hope of eternal life, which God, that cannot lie, promised before the world began"* (Titus 1:2).

"Most of us see change...as something exciting. Yet the fact that Jesus never changes should cause us to find much more rest and peace in His plans. There's no chance of him changing his mind, or of his learning new facts that will cause him to alter his initial decisions. For these reasons I can say He is my shelter, my fortress, my Rock of Ages."   —Cliff Jenkin

For these reasons I, too, can say: "He is my shelter, my fortress and my Rock of Ages."

God's Love

Love can be hard, especially when we have been hurt or are in the process of being hurt. Our human nature leans toward unlovely thoughts, and if not kept in check, they will turn into unlovely words and/or unlovely actions. If loving others came naturally, God would not have had to instruct us to do so: *"And the Lord make you to increase and abound in love one toward another, and toward all men, even as we do toward you"* (1 Thesselonians 3:12). *"Thou shalt love thy neighbor as thyself"* (Galatians 5:14).

The more we can comprehend the Love God has for us, the better we can obey His commandment to extend that love to others. *"That Christ may dwell in your hearts by faith; that ye, being rooted and grounded in love, may be able to comprehend with all saints what is the* **breadth**, *and* **length**, *and* **depth**, *and* **height:**" (Ephesians 3:17-18).

Breadth shows the extent of God's Love; all encompassing, for all people without distinction. *"Out of every kindred, tongue, people, and nation"* (Revelations 5:9).

Length indicates the duration of Christ's Love; love is eternal: *"Chosen before"* (Ephesians 1:4); *"Ages to come"* (Ephesians 1:7).

Depth tells of the condescension of His Love; He reached down from His level to ours. His Love is deeper than our depravity: *"In times past we walked . . ."* (Ephesians 2:1-5).

Height shows God's ultimate and final purpose for us. Love came down to exalt us: *"hath raised us up together, and made us sit together in heavenly places in Christ Jesus"* (Ephesians 2:6). We are in an elevated position before God: *"he is exalted"* (James 1:9).

"And to know the **love** *of Christ, which passeth knowledge, that ye might be filled with all the fulness of God"* (Ephesians 3:19). To know the love of Christ so that our every thought, impulse, value, and goal will be completely dominated by God.

The love of Christ includes all mankind, will last for eternity, reaches down to the most depraved sinner, changes his life, and exalts him to heaven. May these dimensions be real in your life and manifested in your love toward others!

The Power of God to Us Who Believe

There have been days in my life when I have cried to the Lord; "I can't do this."

God's response: *"And what is the **exceeding greatness** of his **power** to us-ward who believe, according to the working of his mighty **power**, Which he wrought in Christ, when he raised him from the dead, and set him at his own right hand in the heavenly places"* (Ephesians 1:19-20).

My God is powerful enough to raise Jesus Christ from the dead!

Stop and think about this: We have at our disposal a power that can overcome any obstacle in our Christian walk!

The first word **power** [*dunamis*] speaks of a raw power, the ability to do wonders, and that which overcomes any resistance. Add "**exceeding greatness**" and it describes a power that goes far beyond what we might ask or think.

The phase "us-ward who believe" tells me this power is directed toward me personally (because of my salvation) so I have no excuse to live a life of up and downs regardless of the circumstances in my life. There is no problem so insurmountable it cannot be solved by our God.

The second word **power** [*ischos*] speaks of strength and physical ability. Add "the **working** of" and "**mighty**" and it describes a power in action showing God's strength. God's strength in my life and God's strength in your life.

"Now unto him that is able to do exceeding abundantly above all that we ask or think, according to the power that worketh in us" (Ephesians. 3:20).

As Christians we have been called to serve and minister. When we doubt our ability to effectively serve the Lord, face difficult tasks, deal with people who hurt us, and/or take on responsibilities which are overwhelming, we must remember it is God's power that "worketh" in us.

"Finally, my brethren, be strong in the Lord, and in the power of His might" (Ephesians 6:10).

My challenge to you and to myself is not to simply recognize God's power, but to claim it and walk the victorious abundant life He desires for us.

Contentment: The Ultimate Acceptance

*"Godliness with **contentment** is great gain"* (1 Timothy 6:6).

*"Be **content** with such things as ye have: for he hath said, I will never leave thee, nor forsake thee"* (Hebrews 13:5).

These past 40 years we have moved many times, lived in various locations, and in different types of housing, including a garage and 1971 Winnebago. We have faced hurt, struggles, and extreme heartache. My goal is to say, like Paul, *"I have learned in whatsoever state I am, therewith to be **content**."* (Philippians. 4:11).

Contentment is the ultimate acceptance of yourself, your surroundings, your past, and your future. As a believer you would think contentment would be effortless, yet it is not an easy task. Satisfaction when we have very real needs; freedom from worry when we have overwhelming concerns; patience while letting God work when pressures abound; happiness despite heartaches caused by past hurts, present tragedies, and an uncertain future.

God chose to teach us to be content as we allow Him to be in control of our life. Circumstances constantly change; therefore contentment is not a *daily* growth process but rather a *moment by moment* growth process.

My challenge to you and myself is to recognize God's sufficiency in our life and to appropriate the spiritual resources provided in Christ through the indwelling Holy Spirit. This will help spur us on to being content regardless of the circumstances, struggles and uncertainties we are facing.

"Not that we are sufficient of ourselves to think anything as of ourselves; but our sufficiency is of God" (2 Corinthians 3:5).
"My grace is sufficient for thee: for my strength is made perfect in weakness. Most gladly therefore will I rather glory in my infirmities, that the power of Christ may rest upon me" (2 Corinthians 12:9).

ALL we experience now should be viewed in light of eternity. If we can trust Him with our eternal state, we can trust him with our today.

Godly Discontentment: "But God. . ."

Contentment—the acceptance of circumstances in our life and viewing them from an eternity with our Lord. However, contentment should NOT apply to our spiritual growth.

*"**But God** will redeem my soul from the power of the grave: for he shall receive me"* (Psalms 49:15).

These two words show the ultimate contrast—from the hopelessness of man to God's provisions and hope: We were once dead, but now we are alive; once we were enemies of God, now we are friends. Once we were aliens, now we are citizens; once lost, now found; once afar off, now drawn near. In times past we were cut off, but now we have access; we were at war with God, now we are at peace; once condemned, now justified. Before Christ we were nothing: a worthless lump of clay, dead in trespasses in sin with no value or purpose.

*"**But God**, who is rich in mercy, for his great love wherewith he loved us, Even when we were dead in sins, hath **quickened us** together with Christ, And hath **raised us up** together, and **made us sit** together in heavenly places in Christ Jesus"* (Ephesians 2:4-6).

God has "**quickened us.**" The same power that raised Jesus Christ from the dead has once and for all made us alive together with Christ.

He has "**raised us up**" from death to new life; a life devoted to God. We are no longer on the level of sin, but rather on a new level with new potential. We are, as Paul calls us, "new creatures." When Christ comes into our life, our life changes. *"My sheep hear my voice, and I know them, and they follow me:"* (John 10:27).

He has "**made us sit**" together in heavenly places. Sitting conveys a place of honor or authority. Christ is seated with honor in the heavenlies, and we have already been exalted with Him.

We should not be content, but rather, we should be dissatisfied with areas of our life that do not align with God's Word. We have been made alive, given new life, and exalted with Him. Let us act like who we are *in Christ*!

"But God:" Two Words that Make the Difference

But *now* **in Christ Jesus** *ye who sometimes were far off are made nigh by the blood of Christ..* [16]*And that he might* <u>reconcile</u> *both unto God in one body by the cross, having slain the enmity thereby:"* (Ephesians 2:13, 16).

While visiting our daughter-in-law Megan this past month, she and I took a walk on a warm day through a graveyard to a lake. As we sat on a bench surrounded by trees enjoying the coolness and the calm, I thought of Adam and Eve in the Garden of Eden, walking with God in the *"cool of the day"* (Genesis 3:8).

The fall ended that communion… **BUT** God sent Jesus Christ to break down this division (Ephesians 2:14). We have been reconciled—changed back to a former state (Colossians 1:21,22). Therefore, we <u>can</u> walk with God in the cool of the day. *"To give light to them that sit in darkness and in the shadow of death, to guide our feet into the way of peace"* (Luke 1:79).

In 1 Peter 5, Peter tells us to *"cast* [this requires action on our part] *all your care on Him for He cares for you"* (v.7). In verse 8 we are directed to be *sober* (serious about spiritual matters) and *vigilant* (carefully watching for possible danger)…**why?** Because Satan is watching, and he wants to cause us to fall under the pressure of our cares—destroying our testimony and making us ineffective Christians (v.9).

"But stand firm in faith" (v.9—believing even when you don't see)…understand, you are not the only one who suffers.

"BUT *the* **GOD** [the two words that make a difference!] *of all grace"* (v.10) has given us eternal life thru Christ Jesus. His grace will cause us to stand strong and calm us—to what end? He will be glorified; He will have rule forever and forever (v.11).

> *Jesus paid it all, all to Him I owe*
> *Sin had left a crimson stain—*
> *He washed it white as snow.*

May you enjoy walking with God in the coolness of the day!

Don't Let Bitterness Take Root

This past year we faced the death of our son, Cliff, which was extremely painful; yet not as devastating as a division within a family unit. Accusations are made, hearts broken, and feelings hurt becoming a breeding ground for bitterness. Bitterness can be anything from simply holding a grudge to the intent to harm. It always opens the door for Satan to work destruction: "...*neither give place* [opportunity] *to the devil*" (Ephesians. 4:27).

We are told, "*Let all* **bitterness**, *and wrath, and anger, and clamor, and evil speaking, be put away from you, with all malice*" (Ephesians 4:31). Bitterness is the end result of suppressed anger and if not dealt with will lead to *wrath* [extreme anger], *clamor* [a crying out against someone], *evil speaking* [damaging speech], and *malice* [desire to do evil]. These are all evil in the sight of God. I can personally attest to how quickly and quietly bitterness creeps in and begins to affect your thoughts and words.

God tells us when we see these characteristics being manifested in our life, we are to "put them away," which means to pick up and carry away, or make a clean sweep. This definitely indicates action on our part: **the choice is ours** and God has given us the power to obey. "*Be kindly affectioned one to another with brotherly love; in honor preferring one another;. . .Bless them which persecute you: bless, and curse not . . .Recompense to no man evil for evil. . .avenge not yourselves, but rather give place unto wrath: for it is written, vengeance is mine; I will repay, saith the Lord. Therefore if thine enemy hunger, feed him; if he thirst, give him drink: for in so doing thou shalt heap coals of fire on his head. Be not overcome of evil, but overcome evil with good*" (Romans 12:9-21).

My challenge to you, and myself, is to not let bitterness take root—recognize it and put it away; then replace it with good and edifying thoughts and speech.

"*Let no corrupt communication proceed out of your mouth, but that which is good to the use of edifying, that it may minister grace unto the hearers*" (Ephesians 4:29).

Abide...Not "Roll with the Punches"

During our many years of missionary service, we have learned that circumstances can change in a heartbeat. In candidate school years ago, one of Brother Art Cunningham's emphases was, "Roll with the punches." I have put that phrase into practice more times than I can count.

Yet I rejoice because God does <u>not</u> "roll with the punches" (John 15:4-10).

Abide is a two-sided coin.. Flip it and God's side will always land face up. God abiding in us! God and His Word are consistent in whatever circumstance we find ourselves in. *"The word of the Lord **endureth** [abide] forever"* (1 Peter 1:25). *"The grass withereth, the flower fadeth: but the word of our God shall **stand** [abide] forever"* (Isaiah 40:8). *"Forever, O Lord, thy word is **settled** [abide] in heaven"* (Psalm 119:89). *"For the truth's sake, which **dwelleth** [abide] in us, and shall be with us forever"* (2 John 1:2).

However, the other side of the coin cannot be ignored—both sides make the coin valuable and usable. As true Christians, we must **abide** in God:

Walk as Christ walked—*"He that saith he abideth in him ought himself also so to walk, even as he walked"* (1 John 2:6).

Think as Christ—*"Let this mind be in you, which was also in Christ Jesus"* (Philippians 2:5).

Act like Christ—*"For I have given you an example, that ye should do as I have done to you"* (John 13:15).

Do NOT live in sin—*"Whosoever abideth in him sinneth not: whosoever sinneth hath not seen him, neither known him"* (1 John 3:6).

Continue in His Word—*"If ye continue (abide) in my word, then are ye my disciples indeed"* (John 8:31).

Obey His Word—*"He that doeth the will of God abideth forever"* (1 John 2:17).

Bears fruit—*"he that abideth in me, and I in him, the same bringeth forth much fruit"* (John 15:5)

My challenge to you is not to "roll with the punches" when it comes to your Christian walk, but rather "**abide**."

I Surrender All

As I recently sang this invitational hymn, I began to focus on the words and what I was saying in my commitment to Jesus:

All to Jesus I surrender, All to Him I freely give;
I will ever love and trust Him, in his presence daily live.
I must love and trust Him and live daily knowing He is ever present!

All to Jesus I surrender, humbly at His feet I bow;
worldly pleasures all forsaken, take me Jesus take me now.
I must live a life consecrated to Him!

All to Jesus I surrender, make me, Savior, wholly Thine;
let me feel Thy Holy Spirit, truly know that Thou art mine.
I must yield to the Holy Spirit and be controlled by Him!

All to Jesus I surrender, Lord, I give myself to Thee;
fill me with Thy love and power, let Thy blessing fall on me.
I must have His love and power to live a victorious Christian life!

"Neither yield ye your members as instruments of unrighteousness unto sin: but yield yourselves unto God, as those that are alive from the dead, and your members as instruments of righteousness unto God" (Romans 6:13). **I must surrender all!**

Every day brings challenges, struggles and hard responsibilities which Satan would like to use to distract us from God's plan for us. However, God wants to use those same challenges, struggles and responsibilities to draw us closer to him, to love and trust Him more, to forsake the world and draw closer to Him, to surrender ourselves wholly yielding to the Holy Spirits leading in our life and to ask for continued filling of His love and power.

I must have His blessings!
"Surely goodness and mercy shall follow me all the days of my life: and I will dwell in the house of the Lord for ever" (Psalms 23:6).

My challenge to myself and to you is "surrender <u>ALL</u>" and be blessed by God.

Preparing the Field

Parts of my lawn needed reseeding so I began raking to clear out the dead grass and break up the top soil. It was hard work, but I knew if I didn't do it right the seeds would fall on hard ground and not germinate; or if some did make it, they would be choked out by the weeds.

I began thinking about Jesus' words in Matthew 13:3-8—*"And he spake many things unto them in parables . . . .Behold, a sower went forth to sow; . . .But other fell into good ground, and brought forth fruit . . ."* It dawned on me that God never asks us to prepare the field.

Bringing men to Christ is a divine/human co-op. **God** prepares the field: *"No man can come to me, except the Father which hath sent me draw him:"* (John 6:44). We sow and water in the power He gives us: *"I have planted, Apollos watered; but God gave the increase"* (1 Corinthians 3:6); *"But ye shall receive power, after that the Holy Ghost is come upon you . . .and ye shall be witnesses unto me . . ."* (Acts 1:8).

I remember sharing the Gospel with a young lady who responded to the invitation one Sunday morning. In the end she said she wasn't ready. I was disappointed I couldn't convince her, however, later that evening she went into her bedroom and prayed to accept Christ. (Today, she is married and growing in the Lord.) What a reminder: it is not about my abilities or inabilities; it is about God drawing them to Himself *(preparing the field)* and enabling me to "sow and water."

The reality is that God doesn't need us, but He desires to use us to bring in the harvest. *"Then saith he unto his disciples, The harvest truly is plenteous, but the labourers are few; Pray ye therefore . . .that he will send forth labourers into his harvest"* (Matthew 9:37-38).

God blesses our faithfulness—He is in charge of the results! Our challenge is to remove the focus from ourselves and go forward "sowing and watering" with confidence.

Count It All As Dung

*"I count all things but loss for the excellency of the knowledge of Christ Jesus my Lord: for whom I have suffered the loss of all things, and do count them but **dung**, that I may win Christ"* (Philippians 3:8).

Paul considered everything of this world as nothing more than the most repulsive word he could think of, dung [something that is not even worthy to be touched or looked at] in comparison to gaining Christ.

I was recently challenged by the question; "are you willing to abandon everything for Christ?" I thought of the song; *I'll Go Where You Want Me to Go*

> *So, trusting my all unto Thy care --*
> *I know Thou loveth me --*
> *I'll do Thy will with a heart sincere,*
> *I'll be what You want me to be.*

Being what 'He wants me to be' includes making the decision to value Him more than what the world has to offer. It requires a self-denying love.

God has given us so much. It is easy to get pre-occupied with things and caught up in activities that we begin to value them more than the One who gave them to us.
Since we do what is important to us -- How much time do we devote to worldly activities in comparison to the time we devote to His Word, prayer, and service?

"And hereby we do know that we know him, if we keep his commandments. He that saith, I know him, and keepeth not his commandments, is a liar, and the truth is not in him. But whoso keepeth his word, in him verily is the love of God perfected: hereby know we that we are in him. He that saith he abideth in him ought himself also so to walk, even as he walked." (1 John 2:3-6)

I challenge myself and you. Do we **really** love the Lord and desire to know Him intimately, esteem Him, value Him over anything the world can offer; count ALL things as dung that we may *"be what He wants us to be"*?

Think On These Things

I had the privilege to teach a week of Bible to Jr./Sr. High girls. One lesson dealt with what God says about our thinking patterns: **All** of our thinking is to be put into the context of God's standard.

Paul describes the unregenerate man as walking in the "vanity of the mind" [full of self with no regard for God] and warns believers not to walk as they walk (Ephesians 4:17). In the simplest terms: **Don't think like the unsaved!**

> *"Finally, brethren, whatsoever things are true, ...honest, ...just, ...pure, ...lovely, ...of good report; if there be any virtue, ...any praise, think on these things."* (Philippians. 4:8)

True - things as they really are, not as they are concealed, falsified, or misrepresented. Not what we imagine they are; not what others say; and not what we feel is the truth.

Honest [gravity] - things that are serious, uplifting, and majestic. This has to do with our reaction and treatment of God's Word. "My heart standeth in awe of God's Word" (Psalm 119:161).

Just - upright and righteous. We should think on God's righteous acts. *"The righteousness of God which is by faith of Jesus Christ unto all and upon all them that believe"* (Romans 3:22). If we focus on God and what He has done for us through Christ, our minds would be too occupied to think negative.

Pure - cleanness, chastity. Because Christ is pure, our thought patterns should be pure. *"The wisdom from above is first pure..."* (James 3:17).

Lovely - acceptable, pleasing and amiable. This word has also been translated as "that which calls forth love." It is not lying, cursing, gossiping, losing our temper, or that which causes unlovely behavior.

Good Report - positive words. Think (and talk) about things that are positive and constructive. Do not dwell on past mistakes, sin, or regrets.

Paul wants to be all-inclusive, so he adds: if there be any **virtue** [excellence of any kind; the highest good of humanity] and if there be any **praise** [things that give God praise] then **think on these things**. *"For as he thinketh in his heart, so is he"* (Proverbs 23:7).

Make This Day Count

Rejoice. . . This could be the year Jesus comes and takes us home!

"Wherefore he saith, Awake thou that sleepest, and arise from the dead" (Ephesians 5:14-16).

Believers are being told;
Awake not from sleeping physically, but to be alert and ready for the challenges and commands of living an effective Christian life.

Walk circumspectly *not as fools, but as wise.*
An example of this would be how we walk after we have dropped a glass on a tile floor; it shatters into tiny pieces and is thrown all across the room. We carefully examine each step as we go to get a broom or vacuum to clean it up so not to step on a tiny shard of glass.

Redeeming the time, *because the days are evil*; not simply making the most of our time but making it ours and using it correctly. We are not to be dwelling in the past, wishing the day to be over or focusing only on tomorrow. God wants us to consider each and every moment as an opportunity for growth, service and witness. A fool wastes time...the wise invests it.

The key to all of this is back in verse 14; **Christ shall give thee light**. He will illumine His Word that much more to our hearts and mind so we can walk circumspectly and redeem the time.

Just think about it: we have the Light who gives us the light. There is NO reason we need to walk through this life wishing for tomorrow because we can't handle today or living in the past because the future looks hopeless.

Yes, this could be the year!
"Therefore let us not sleep, as do others; but let us watch and be sober. . . let us, who are of the day, be sober, putting on the breastplate of faith and love; and for an helmet, the hope of salvation" (1 Thessalonians 5:6.8).

Make this day count for all eternity!

I Am Who I AM

We are the sum total of our experiences. Our characters are forged in the fires we did not build and there's little we can do to change them.

The world says: "We are what we are and there is nothing we can do about it." "If my mom beat me with a broom, I can't help but beat my kids with a broom." "My mom was a yeller, so I am a yeller."

Several years into my Christian life, I was still in the mindset that I was -just like my father-: I did not wear my emotions on my sleeve; I avoided hugs and preferred not to have to inter-act with lots of people.

As God worked in my life, I began to understand that although I 'take after' my earthly father, I could not use it as an excuse in how I lived my Christian life. The verse God impressed upon my mind and which became my life verse is:
"I am crucified with Christ:nevertheless I live; yet not I, but Christ liveth in me:and the life which I now live in the flesh I live by the faith of the Son of God, who loved me, and gave himself for me" (Galatians 2:20).

Our characters may have been built in fires we did not build, But WE CAN change!!! This is a promise from God as we **yield**-commit ourselves - daily to HIM.
"I beseech you therefore, brethren, by the mercies of God, that ye present [yield] your bodies a living sacrifice, holy, acceptable unto God, which is your reasonable service. And be not conformed to this world: but be ye transformed by the renewing of your mind, that ye may prove what is that good, and acceptable, and perfect, will of God" (Romans 12:1-2).

I warn you, God will take you out of your comfort zone. It may even hurt as He molds and shapes you into a usable vessel.

May we then be able to say; "I am who I am IN CHRIST."

What Are Our Orders?

Because our son-in-law, Dan, is a major in the Army, I have been on military bases and have witnessed soldiers in training. However, you do not need to know someone in the military in order to understand the importance of Paul's instructions to Timothy. *"This charge I commit unto thee, son Timothy, according to the prophecies which went before on thee, that thou by them mightest war a good warfare"* (1 Timothy 1:18).

All Christians, we have been given a mission. We are in a battle and we are to "wage a good warfare." Christ has secured the victory; yet we will still face the enemy.

God has given us clear orders.

Endure Hardship. *"Endure hardness, as a good soldier of Jesus Christ"* (2 Timothy 2:3). Being a Christian soldier is not easy. To endure hardship literally means to suffer evil and affliction. It demands preparation; preparation through study and prayer.

Take Orders. The soldier who does not submit to authority and the "chain of command" will not last long in the military. Likewise, we must be in submission to Christ and His Word. We will have to give account for the leadership He has placed us in.

Identify the Enemy. *"For we wrestle not against flesh and blood, but against principalities, against powers, against the rulers of the darkness of this world, against spiritual wickedness in high places"* (Ephesians 6:12). We must not forget we have a strong enemy: Satan. He rules along with evil spirits which control this world through ignorance, misery and sin.

Kill the enemy and destroy his fortifications. Negotiations are not an option. *"For though we walk in the flesh, we do not war after the flesh: For the weapons of our warfare are not carnal, but mighty through God to the pulling down of strong hold"* (2 Corinthians 10:3-4).

So the Christian soldier **must** be skillful in using the weapons God has provided for the war.

Get Your Gear Together and Move Out

We have our orders - now "Get your gear together and move out." Along with those orders God gives us the **enablement** and **equipment** to fight. Ephesians 4:24 *"put on the new man"*. We are taking to ourselves qualities and characteristics that are now part of our very nature: righteousness and holiness (Colossians 3:12; 2 Peter 1:4).

*"Put on the whole armor of God, that ye may be able to **stand against** the wiles of the devil. Wherefore take unto you the whole armor of God, that ye may be able to **withstand** in the evil day, and having done all, to stand"* (Ephesians 6:11, 13).

Stand against and **Withstand:** Militarily speaking, no battle, no war, can be won by defense alone. God not only wants us to stand our ground and face the enemy, but He wants us to resist and land blows of our own with the Word of God.

We can only be victorious in this spiritual war if we clothe ourselves with ALL **the weapons** and leave them on for the duration of the conflict -- until we go home to be with The Lord.

Girdle of Truth: God's Word is the foundation of our lives. Truth affects our thinking, our confidence, our choices and our response to difficulties.

Breastplate of righteousness: The imputed righteousness of Christ, which produces holy living, protects important areas including our testimony, confidence, peace, joy.

Feet shod with the preparation of the Gospel of peace: We are to be ready to do whatever is needed because we have peace with God [judicial] and the peace of God [experiential]. While the world is in turmoil, we can feel relaxed, assured and confident.

Shield of Faith: We live by faith; what God says He will do, He will do.

Helmet of salvation: Our "salvation" protects us from Satan's attacks on the mind: doubt & discouragement.

Sword of the Spirit: The word of God is our only offensive weapon to attack all untruth.

May we be able to say: *"I have fought a good fight, I have finished my course, I have kept the faith"* (2 Timothy 4:7).

Watch

I was watching the news this morning as they were trying to apprehend the second Boston Marathon bomber. They kept looping the same scene over and over: of officers waiting in anticipation for what might happen; FBI ready to draw their weapons; and a special SWAT team member with an automatic rifle aimed at something. Words from the reporters—keeping an eye on, alert, in a ready state—reminded me of Paul's words to the Corinthians and ultimately to us: *"**Watch** ye, stand fast in the faith, quit you like men, be strong"* (1 Corinthians 16:13).

Watch literally means to refrain from sleep, however in the spiritual sense, watch means to be attentive and vigilant. Jesus wasn't just concerned that the disciples fell asleep; he was more concerned that they were not being vigilant and watching. *"And he cometh unto the disciples, and findeth them asleep, and saith unto Peter, What, could ye not watch with me one hour? **Watch** and pray, that ye enter not into temptation: the spirit indeed is willing, but the flesh is weak"* (Matthew 26:40-41).

I wonder how many times I am lulled to sleep by the blessings of Christianity forgetting that *"our adversary the devil, as a roaring lion, walketh about, seeking whom he may devour"* (1 Peter 5:8).

As Christians we need to be attentive to spiritual things, to stand for Christ at all times, never giving an inch concerning the Christian faith; we are to stay strong and never quit. *"Therefore let us not sleep, as do others; but let us **watch** and be sober"* (1 Thessalonians 5:6). *"But the end of all things is at hand: be ye therefore sober, and watch unto prayer"* (1 Peter 4:7).

My challenged to myself and you: *"Watch therefore, for you do not know when the master of the house is coming—in the evening, at midnight, at the crowing of the rooster, or in the morning lest, coming suddenly, he find you sleeping. And what I say to you, I say to all: Watch!"* (Mark 13:36, 37)

You Are Planted

A few months ago my mom called to let me know she bought six rose bushes as my Christmas gift, and that they would be delivered at the right time for planting. Sure enough, one day earlier this spring there sat a large package at my front door. Since I was unable to plant them right away because of all the rain we were experiencing (plus I had no idea where I was going to plant them!) I left them in their individual plastic bag and placed them in our cool, dark garage knowing they could not grow unless I planted them.

I potentially could make a mistake on when and where I plant my rose bushes, but God makes no mistakes. *"I am fearfully and wonderfully made. . . The days fashioned for me . . . How precious also are Your thoughts to me, O God! How great is the sum of them!" (*Psalms 139:13-18).

We are not where we are by blind chance, and God has determined our days. *"And hath made of one blood all nations of men for to dwell on all the face of the earth, and hath determined the times before appointed, and the bounds of their habitation"* (Acts 17:26).

When we accept Christ as Savior, we are translated. *"Who hath delivered us from the power of darkness, and hath translated us into the kingdom of his dear Son"* (Colossians 1:13). We are still plagued with thorns and thistles, we still face droughts, and we still experience storms. However: **Each trial we go through is a means for spiritual growth. Each temptation we face allows God to grow us.**

We have not been taken out of the world and its influence, but rather we have been given the Holy Spirit and the Word of God so that we might *"not be conformed to this world: but be transformed by the renewing of your mind, that ye may prove what is that good, and acceptable, and perfect, will of God"* (Romans 12:2).

Praise God for where He has planted you. Incidentally, I planted my roses in an old fire pit and they are growing beautifully.

God Expects Us to Grow!

"For every one that uses milk is unskillful in the word of righteousness: for he is a babe. But strong meat [solid food] *belongeth to them that are of full age, even those who by reason of use have their senses exercised to discern both good and evil"* (Hebrews 5:13-14).

God not only expects growth, He provides for it! *"According as his divine power hath given unto us all things that pertain unto life and godliness. . . . .For if these things be in you, and abound, they make you that ye shall neither be barren nor unfruitful in the knowledge of our Lord Jesus Christ"* (2 Peter 1:3-8).

I like to take credit for my roses growing and blooming, but I know it is the water and the sun which makes them strong. Likewise, **the Holy Spirit of God causes growth as we feed and nourish Him with the Word of God** *". . .having heard the word, keep it, and bring forth fruit with patience"* (Luke 8:15).

Living a victorious **FRUITFUL** Christian life is supernatural. *"Abide in me, and I in you. As the branch cannot **bear fruit** of itself, except it abide in the vine; no more can ye, except ye abide in me. I am the vine , ye are the branches: He that abideth in me, and I in him, the same **bringeth forth much fruit**: for without me ye can do nothing"* (John 15:4-6). It is Christ *in us* that makes it possible.

What kind of fruit? Strength (Psalm 1:3), converts (John 4:36; 15:16), worship (Hebrews 13:5), wholesome conduct (Romans 6:22; Luke 6:43-44), and the essence of Christ's character (Galatians 5:22-23).

"And that which fell among thorns are they which, when they have heard, go forth and are choked with cares and riches and pleasures of this life, and bring NO FRUIT to perfection" (Luke 8:14).

The choice is ours!

I Just Want to Praise Him

As the deer . . . that song is going through my head as we sit here in Montana, early in the morning by the fire, watching three doe and two bucks in velvet cross through our property stopping along the way to check us out (and long enough for me to get my camera). How I rejoice in God's beautiful creation and His wonderful kindness to allow us to enjoy it. *"And God made the beast of the earth after his kind, and cattle after their kind, and everything that creepeth upon the earth after his kind:* **and God saw that it was good"** (Genesis 1:25).

When Bill and I planned this year's trip to work on the cabin, our goal was to start working on the inside: perhaps the electric, maybe the floor. As we have seen in the past, God brings folks along who are exactly what we need.

Bill loves to invite folks to come and help on the cabin with the promise that "if you come to work, we will feed you and put you up". Many have heard it, and a few have taken us up on it including the family here this week.

After Bill made this offer at a Sportsman's Dinner in Illinois, two young men asked their dad; "why can't we do that?" So the plans were made for them to make the trip west along with their Uncle to help work on the cabin. We did not ask for their abilities or expertise, just thankful for the young 'muscle'. The first day we found out that Ken, the dad, a financial advisor, was skilled as a framer. Therefore, the next trip to town was to order all the lumber for framing the inside walls. WOW! That was not even on our list.

"By him therefore let us offer the sacrifice of praise to God continually, that is, the fruit of our lips giving thanks to his name" (Hebrews 13:15).

I get so excited to see how God shows Himself in what we consider just ordinary activities and plans. I just want to PRAISE HIM!

What's In a Name?

What's in a name? Our oldest, William Scott IV, is named after his dad, who was named after his dad, who was named after his dad. Our daughter, Debby Kay, is named after my sister who was killed when I was three months pregnant. The twins, Clifford Marvin and Clinton Michael, have no particular significance except Cliff has my father's name as his middle name. My grandchildren all have names chosen for a particular reason: Hunter Riley, Sydney Nicole, Lexus Paige, William Alexander V, Maxwell Kent, Stetson Cole, Slate Dante, and Shiloh Benjamin Clifford.

So how important is a name? In the Old Testament, names were very significant in the Jewish thinking. In the New Testament, names reflect character. The names of God: God, Jesus, Christ, Savior, Lord, I AM, the Alpha and the Omega, and Almighty (to name just a few) are significant. Each tells some aspect of His character and being.

We, too, as believers in Jesus Christ have names which should characterize us:

Saint—one who has been set apart. We are not dependent on our works, but on the Grace of God. (1 Corinthians 1:2)
Servant—one who is altogether consumed in the will of the other; also translated Slave, meaning that everything we do, we should do with Jesus in mind; to bring glory to Him. (John 12:26)
Friend—someone for which there is a tender affection. (John 15:14)
Christian—of the party of Christ. Although it is used lightly today, this name should describe someone who acts like Christ, who stands for righteousness and doesn't fit in with everyone else. (Acts 26:28)
Fellow Citizens—one who has full protections and rights. We have great privileges since we are citizens of a far greater country than where we live physically. (Ephesians 2:19)

Take time to search and study the names of God, as well as what we are called as believers in Jesus Christ. You will be blessed as well as challenged.

God always lives up to his name. Are we living up to ours?

Where's My Focus?

I would love to say my focus on the Lord is 100% every day. However, during more times than I would like to admit, while facing difficult situations, my initial focus is on how I am going to respond to it or/and how am I going to get through it.

I discovered this to be so true when I lost my wallet containing credit cards, bank cards, driver's license, Indian tribal ID, and my concealed weapon license. Panic prevailed before I focused on the Lord.

Too often it takes a sleepless night before I yield to the Holy Spirit and *"turn my eyes upon Jesus."*

Focusing on Jesus may not change my circumstances, but my response can change. I think of Jesus not opening His mouth to answer his tormentors: *"He was oppressed, and he was afflicted, yet he opened not his mouth:"* (Isaiah 53:7), and of his word to His Father in Luke 22:42 saying, *"Father, if thou be willing, remove this cup from me: nevertheless* **not my will, but thine**, *be done."*

Time in the Word of God helps us realize what an amazing life we have in Him. He knows all about whatever it is causing our frustration or pain, and He can do something about it. This "something" may be removing it but more often the "something" is to change us. *"And be not conformed to this world; but be ye transformed by the renewing of your mind that ye may prove what is that good and acceptable, and perfect, will of God"* (Romans 12:2).

When we understand that God uses all difficulties to perfect His children, we can take our focus off the difficulties and experience peace (and from personal experience, I know this is a decision: it is not automatic).

Focus on HIM and you can't help but *"Turn your eyes upon Jesus; look full in His wonderful face, and the things of earth will grow strangely dim, in the light of His Glory and Grace."*

Just Passing Through

I am not one to get caught up in the politics of today, but what I hear and see regarding our country is depressing. I was recently reminded that we are not citizens of this world trying to get to heaven; rather, we are citizens of heaven just trying to get through this world.

God's people were "strangers" in the land of Egypt (Acts 13:17). Those who died in faith recognized they were "strangers" and "pilgrims" on the earth (Hebrews 11:13). In 1 Peter 2:11, believers, as well are called "strangers" and "pilgrims."

"Now therefore ye are no more strangers and foreigners, but fellow citizens with the saints, and of the household of God" (Ephesians 2:19).

As citizens of the United States we have been given great privileges, yet we are only wanderers or refugees *[strangers]*. Although we live in and enjoy the protection of this country, our citizenship is elsewhere *[foreigners]*. We have a common citizenship in Christ *[fellow citizens with the saints and of the household of God]*. We have even greater privileges in Christ. Which one will we focus on? Where will we put our energies: political reform, social change? I am not saying we should hide our heads in the sand regarding the political climate and changes around us; but realize change comes one person at a time.

Our focus and our energies need to be placed on the priorities of Jesus Christ. *"This is a faithful saying, and worthy of all acceptation, that Christ Jesus came into the world to save sinners"* (1 Timothy 1:15).
"For the son of man is come to seek and to save that which was lost" (Luke 19:10).

Even Paul says preaching the Gospel had priority over everything else he taught: *"For I delivered unto you first of all that which I also received, how that Christ died for our sins according to the scriptures"* (1 Corinthians 15:3).

So as we face the day to day challenges and the uncertainties of our future government, take heart – we are just passing through.

Only Begotten Son

Jesus Christ is not God's "only son." He is God's "Only Begotten [uniquely born] Son." He is the radiance of the glory of God; the exact imprint of God's nature. **God Himself in the flesh.**

"Hath in these last days spoken unto us by his Son, whom he hath appointed heir of all things, by whom also he made the worlds; Who being the brightness of his glory, and the express image of his person, and upholding all things by the word of his power, when he had by himself purged our sins, sat down on the right hand of the Majesty on high; Being made so much better than the angels, as he hath by inheritance obtained a more excellent name than they. For unto which of the angels said he at any time, Thou art my Son, this day have I begotten thee? And again, I will be to him a Father, and he shall be to me a Son? And again, when he bringeth in the firstbegotten into the world, he saith, And let all the angels of God worship him" (Hebrews 1:2-6)

We celebrate the birth of Christ – *"firstborn among many brethren"* (Romans 8:29). Who are these many brethren? *"...to as many as received Him to them gave He the power to become the sons of God"* (John 1:2). By the sovereign act of God all who receive Him are called the God's children, joint heirs with Christ. This includes me, and I trust includes you.

As the firstborn, Jesus Christ has set the example for us: *"But thou, O man of God, flee these things; and follow after righteousness, godliness, faith, love, patience, meekness"* (1 Timothy 6:11).

Paul tells Timothy, *"Let no man despise thy youth; but be thou an example of the believers, in word, in conversation, in charity, in spirit, in faith, in purity"* (1 Timothy 2:12).

People must see in us a growing, victorious Christian. May we humbly say with Paul, *"be ye followers of me, even as I also am of Christ"* (1 Corinthians 11:1).

Focus: Past, Present and Future

Whenever Bill serves communion, he reminds folks to: 1) **look back** with appreciation; 2) **look within** with examination; and 3) **look ahead** with anticipation.

Looking back with appreciation. Not only my appreciation for what God has done regarding my salvation and the transformation of my life (Gal. 2:20), but also my appreciation for His active working in my life throughout the year. Just as newspapers and TV do specials looking back at the events that shaped the previous year, I look back with appreciation for how His love and power were manifested in the events that shaped my life in 2013.

Because of His promises and His faithfulness, I can **look ahead with anticipation**. I will one day see Jesus face to face; through death or the rapture. It is a sure thing! In the meantime, I can move forward facing the future with great courage and confidence: *"The Lord will perfect that which concerneth me"* (Psalm 138:8). *"In all thy ways acknowledge him and He shall direct thy path"* (Prov. 3:6). *"But they that wait upon the Lord shall renew their strength; they shall mount up with wings as eagles; they shall run, and not be weary; and they shall walk, and not faint"* (Isaiah 40:31).

That brings me to the here and now; **looking within with examination**. *"Search me, O God, and know my heart: try me, and know my thoughts: And see if there be any wicked way in me, and lead me in the way everlasting"* (Psalms 139:23-24).

Are my actions and reactions today being influenced more by the things of the world or my relationship with Christ? *"And be not conformed to this world: but be ye transformed by the renewing of your mind"* (Romans 12:2). *"Wherefore seeing we also are compassed about with so great a cloud of witnesses, let us lay aside every weight, and the sin which doth so easily beset us, [past] and let us run with patience the race that is set before us [present], Looking unto Jesus the author and finisher of our faith [future]"* (Hebrews 12:1-2).

May we all make an impact for Christ TODAY!

Reflecting Our Identity

While in Montana this past month, we had the privilege to attend the memorial service of a dear friend. The message at the grave site reminded us that it wasn't what Roger **did**, but rather **who** Roger was. He had a clear testimony of salvation and it was **his identity in Christ** that counted.

I listened to story after story of how Roger used the things he loved—music, horses, and the great outdoors—to bring Glory to God It was clear that what he did in his life reflected his identity in Christ. One man shared how upon their return from the mission field in Africa, his boys were having a difficult time adjusting. Roger invited them to accompany him on a trail ride in the mountains, making a lasting impression on them. Another shared how Roger would counsel him as they sat around the campfire on the trail.

Roger touched Bill's and my life as well. Roger led the singing in his local church and while visiting our church plants in Florida a few times, he would offer to lead the singing. Several years ago, he and his wife, Pat, took Bill and me into the Bob Marshall Wilderness on horseback for a week. It was a once in a lifetime experience and adventure!

As the testimonies went on, I was struck with God's loving kindness in allowing Roger's love for horses and his love for the outdoors to be used as a ministry platform. Serving God and enjoying life....enjoying life and serving God; they can and should go together!

"Whether therefore ye eat, or drink, or whatsoever ye do, do all to the glory of God" (1 Corinthians 1:31). *"According as his divine power hath given unto us all things that pertain unto life and godliness, through the knowledge of him that hath called us to glory and virtue"* (2 Peter 1:3). *"I am come that they might have life and that they might have it more abundantly"* (John 10:10).

Can your love for _____ (you fill in the blank) be used for God? Nothing in your life is a waste unless you refuse to let God use it.

A Glimpse of Answered Prayer

"Praying always with all prayer and supplication in the Spirit, being watchful to this end with all perseverance and supplication for all the saints." (Ephesians 6:18)

Last month we were in Illinois for a Sportsman Dinner and Sunday services. Knowing the weather in Michigan was questionable for the journey home, the pastor and wife assured us they would be praying. Weather was great all through Illinois and going around Chicago proved to be no problem at all. As we began getting closer to the Michigan border, I texted the pastor's wife to let her know the weather was changing and, of course, it was affecting the roads. She texted back; "We will pray." Another dear sister in the Lord was concerned about us and had texted us that she, too, would be praying as we traveled.

No more than five minutes later, we hit a patch of ice. In what seemed like slow motion, we spun around 360 degrees. I thought for sure Bill was going to gain control, but abandoned that thought when we did another 180 degree spin and began sliding backwards. Out my window I could see the cable barrier getting closer and knew we were going to hit. The cable caused extensive damage to the car, but it prevented us from going into the ditch and being buried in deep snow (we saw many others in that predicament all the way home). We finally came to a stop and looking up we saw headlights of a semi. However, by now, we were off the road and out of danger. Since no one else was involved and the car was running, we spun another 180 and headed home leaving a piece of the back fender lying there alongside the road.

The first thing that entered my mind as we continued home was how asking for traveling mercies is not a trivial thing. Although it is repeated over and over again, we should not become weary of asking. God gave me a glimpse of His protection and the importance of that particular prayer.

"Continue in prayer, and watch in the same with thanksgiving." (Colossians 4:2)

Called To Witness

In Acts 22, Paul had a great opportunity to share his testimony. You would think there would have been some 'oohs' and 'aahs' while listening to the transformation God made in his life. But no, not only was the audience not impressed; they wanted him done away with.

Paul takes another opportunity to share his testimony before King Agrippa in Act 26. King Agrippa says *"you almost persuaded me to be a Christian"* (v 28). Paul shared his heart, and in both cases, Christ was rejected; yet Paul continued to do what God instructed him to do.

Paul was chosen so he would know and do God's Will which included telling what great things God had done in his life. *"And he (Ananias) said, (to Paul) the God of our fathers hath chosen thee, that thou shouldest know his will, and see that Just One, and shouldest hear the voice of his mouth. For thou shalt be his witness unto all men of what thou hast seen and heard"* (Acts 22:14-15).

Everyone has a dynamic testimony! We always emphasized to our children that it doesn't require a great deal of sin in your life prior to receiving Christ for your salvation experience to be miraculous. If you are excited about your salvation, others will be excited about it.

We are no different than Paul: <u>God has chosen us and has called us to be His witnesses.</u>
"Ye have not chosen me, but I have chosen you, and ordained you, that ye should go and bring forth fruit, and that your fruit should remain: that whatsoever ye shall ask of the Father in my name, he may give it you." (John 15:16).

I have been reminded, and I challenge you: 1) be excited to share your testimony and 2) do not be discouraged - leave the results to the Lord.

"No man can come to me, except the Father which hath sent me draw him . . . "(John 6:44).

Christ's Strength

"I can do all things through Christ which strengtheneth me"
(Philippians 4:13).

This is a familiar verse and one that we grab hold of when faced with challenges or what we perceive as impossible pursuits.

This past month, while traveling, we were able to visit the Creation Museum in Kentucky. As we walked through the exhibits, one grabbed my attention. It was a mannequin representing Paul sitting at a desk writing a letter. It wasn't the writing tool that drew my attention but the simple act of him writing. My mind went back to a few days prior when I had to address several envelopes 'by hand'. I had a comfortable pen, but my hand still got tired. Did Paul think *"I can do all things through Christ which strengtheneth me"* as he wrote hour after hour? Paul was well versed in the Old Testament and I have to believe that God brought to Paul's mind the truth of His Word.

"The LORD God is my strength" (Habakkuk 3:19).
"The LORD is my rock, and my fortress, and my deliverer; my God, my strength" (Psalm 18:2).
"The LORD is the strength of my life" (Psalms 27:1).
"The LORD is my strength" (Psalms 28:7).

Regardless of the difficulty of the task, we can put on Christ's strength: from opening our eyes in the morning to closing them at night. The very love that is required of us –*"Thou shalt love the Lord thy God with all thy heart, and with all thy soul, and with all thy strength , and with all thy mind; and thy neighbour as thyself"* (Luke 10:27) -can only be accomplished because Christ gives us the strength. His strength becomes our strength!

It does not matter what the day holds - a simple task we face or a difficult one we need to tackle– we can do ALL things through Christ who is our strength and strengthens us. A double whammy!

I have been reminded and I remind you: Each and every day gives us opportunities to experience the strength of God in our lives.

Authority

Our children attended a Christian school which had some strict rules regarding dress and behavior. Rather than criticize and complain, we taught them that all their lives they would be under someone's authority and there will always be rules and regulations to follow.

True Christianity is not a set of rules and regulations; however, there are certain truths and principals we must apply if we are to live a victorious life in Christ.
*"For the grace of God that bringeth salvation hath appeared to all men, Teaching us that, denying ungodliness and worldly lusts, we should live soberly, righteously, and godly, in this present world; Looking for that blessed hope, and the glorious appearing of the great God and our Saviour Jesus Christ; Who gave himself for us, that he might redeem us from all iniquity, and purify unto himself a peculiar people, zealous of good works. These things speak, and exhort, and rebuke with all **authority**"* (Titus 2:11-14).
Authority here means a command or decree that is to be done decidedly, without doubt, without compromise and without keeping anything back. Not simply advice but as the requirement of God.

Jesus Christ taught with authority: *"And they were astonished at his doctrine: for he taught them as one that had **authority**"* (Mark 1:22). Also see Mark 6:2.
Authority here means a privilege; a delegated influence and it also has with it the connotation of having freedom. It has been translated elsewhere in Scripture as liberty, power or strength.

The disciples were given this authority: *"Then he called his twelve disciples together, and gave them power and authority over all devils, and to cure diseases"* (Luke 9:1). Also see Mark 6:7.

We have been given this authority: *"For the Son of man is as a man taking a far journey, who left his house, and gave **authority** to his servants, and to every man his work, and commanded the porter to watch"* (Mark 13:34).

We have been given **authority** [the command to do so without compromise] to speak, exhort and rebuke with all **authority** [freedom and power]. Wow, a double whammy!

We Shall Know Him

A few years ago, I set a goal to get to know Jesus Christ better. The whole essence of who Jesus Christ is is the anchor for a victorious Christian walk.

Getting to know Jesus Christ better gave me a picture of myself:

- Who I was (and can still act like): *"Wherein in time past ye walked according to the course of this world, according to the prince of the power of the air, Among whom also we all had our conversation in times past in the lusts of our flesh, fulfilling the desires of the flesh and of the mind; and were by nature the children of wrath"* (Ephesians 2:2-3).

- What He did for me: *"But God, who is rich in mercy, for his great love wherewith he loved us, Even when we were dead in sins, hath quickened us together with Christ, And hath raised us up together, and made us sit together in heavenly places in Christ Jesus"* (Ephesians 2:4-6).

- The kind of life I can live if I simply abide in Him: *"That in the ages to come he might shew the exceeding riches of his grace in his kindness toward us . . . For we are his workmanship, created in Christ Jesus unto good work . . ."* (Ephesians 2:7, 10).
  "If ye abide in me, and my words abide in you, ye shall ask what ye will, and it shall be done unto you. . .These things have I spoken unto you, that my joy might remain in you, and that your joy might be full" (John 15:7,11).

One day this journey of getting to know Jesus Christ will end when I see Him face to face. *"Beloved, now are we the sons of God, and it doth not yet appear what we shall be: but we know that, when he shall appear, we shall be like him; for we shall see him as he is"* (1 John 3:2).

"I trust you are, as I am, looking forward to that day; whether in death or the rapture, when we shall KNOW HIM and the power of His resurrection" (Philippians 3:10).

Choices

While visiting Dublin Christian Academy in May we were able to see the classroom building named after Cliff (Jenkin Hall) - and on the wall in large letters we read:

> Life is choices
> Choices have consequences
> Make right choices
> C. Jenkin

After thinking about it, I could not come up with any area of life in which we don't make choices. God purposely created us with a free will so we can freely choose Him and freely choose to love Him in the midst of so many options and oppositions. The most important choices in life revolve around what we do with Jesus.

Choice:

- *"What shall we do . . . Jesus answered and said unto them, This is the work of God, that ye believe on him whom he hath sent"* (John 6:28-29).

There are only two consequences for this choice:
"Whosoever believeth in him should not perish, but have <u>everlasting life</u>. . . He that believeth on him is not condemned: but he that believeth not <u>is condemned</u> already, because he hath not believed in the name of the only begotten Son of God" (John 3:16, 18).

Choice:

- *"Choose you this day whom ye will serve"* (Joshua 24:15).

- *"No one can serve two masters . . . You cannot serve God and mammon"* (Matthew 6:24).

- *"And whatsoever ye do in word or deed, do all in the name of the Lord Jesus,"* (Colossians 3:17).

- *"Whether therefore ye eat, or drink, or whatsoever ye do, do all to the glory of God"* (1 Corinthians 10:31).

There are numerous consequences; so I challenge you to do a study and discover for yourself the consequences of an obedient life.

- *"And whatsoever we ask, we receive of him, because we keep his commandments, and do those things that are pleasing in his sight"* (1 John 3:22).

- *"If ye abide in me, and my words abide in you, ye shall ask what ye will, and it shall be done unto you"* (John 15:7).

God has the authority yet He does not demand that we honor Him. When we understand the consequences of loving Him, submitting to Him and obeying Him, it helps us to make the right choice in our words and deeds bringing Him glory.

Faithfulness (Part 1)

As you read this, Bill and my time in Montana has come to an end. Our plan to spend more time working on the cabin was just that "our plan". The death of my dad the day we arrived changed those plans. Yet, the faithfulness our Lord in allowing us to accomplish what He had planned cannot be overlooked.

God is the perfect definition of **faithfulness**: dependable, loyal and stable. Since we are being conformed to the very image of his Son, Jesus Christ; God expects us to be faithful.

God's faithfulness should be reflected in our lives:
"Moreover it is required in stewards, that a man be found faithful" (1 Corinthians 4:2).

Faith is the medium of exchange in doing business with God:
"But without faith it is impossible to please him" (Hebrews 11:6).

We are to be faithful with what gives us
"As every man hath received the gift, even so minister the same one to another, as good stewards of the manifold grace of God" (1 Peter 4:10).

The parable of the talents in Matthew 5:14-30 is connected to the previous parable of the ten virgins as it illustrates how to prepare for the Lord's coming. It has nothing to do with our wealth, but rather increasing what God has entrusted us with including our knowledge, abilities, talents and gifts (Luke 12:48) Each of us according to our own ability is expected to use what we have been given, including material things, for the honor of Christ. The servants in Matthew used what their master gave them to their fullest and they were ready to give a joyful account when their master came and called for them.

God's faithful stewards have something to show for their faithfulness:
"Who is a wise man and endued with knowledge among you? let him shew out of a good conversation his works with meekness of wisdom" (James 3:13).

God equips us to be faithful

The faith to begin our walk with Christ is given to us by God:
For by grace are ye saved through faith: and that not of yourselves: it is the gift of God: (Ephesians 2:8). *"Looking unto Jesus the author and finisher of our faith"* (Hebrews 12:2).

The faith to walk our walk is given to us by God; *"according as God hath dealt to every man the measure of faith"* (Romans 12:3).

       -through the Word of God: *"So then faith cometh by hearing, and hearing by the word of God"* (Romans 10:17). The word of God is worthy of our study, of our close and careful investigation: *"We have also a more sure word of prophecy; whereunto ye do well that ye take heed"* (2 Peter 1:19).

       -enabled by the Holy Spirit
He has given us the Holy Spirit to enable us to demonstrate our faith: *"But the fruit of the Spirit is love, joy, peace, longsuffering, gentleness, goodness, faith, Meekness, temperance:"* (Galatians 5:22, 23).

May God find us faithful in our daily walk with Him.

I Have Kept the Faith (Part 2)

God, the very definition of faithfulness, equips us to be faithful; from the beginning of our walk with Christ to the very end of our lives. His Word and The Holy Spirit work together to enable us to demonstrate our faith. Therefore, God's faithfulness should be reflected in our lives.

Spiritual growth

"But grow in the grace and knowledge of our Lord and Savior Jesus Christ" (2 Peter 3:18).

"As newborn babes, desire the sincere milk of the word, that ye may grow thereby" (1 Peter 2:2).

"For every one that useth milk is unskillful in the word of righteousness: for he is a babe. But strong meat (solid food) belongeth to them that are of full age . . . " (Hebrews 5:13-14).

Being Fruitful

"I am the vine, ye are the branches: He that abideth in me, and I in him, the same bringeth forth much fruit:" (John 15:5-6).

"But he that received seed into the good ground is he that heareth the word, and understandeth it; which also beareth fruit, and bringeth forth, some an hundredfold, some sixty, some thirty" (Matthew 13:23).

"But that on the good ground are they, which in an honest and good heart, having heard the word, keep it, and bring forth fruit with patience" (Luke 8:15).

"For the fruit of the Spirit is in all goodness and righteousness and truth" (Ephesians 5:9).

"But the fruit of the Spirit is love, joy, peace, longsuffering, gentleness, goodness, faith, Meekness, temperance" (Galatians 5:22-23).

Impact on other's lives

"Wherefore seeing we also are compassed about with so great a cloud of witnesses , let us lay aside every weight, and the sin which doth so easily beset us, and let us run with patience the race that is set before us" (Hebrews 12:1).

May we be faithful as we prepare for His coming to take us home? *"I have fought a Good fight, I have finished the race, I have kept the faith "* (2 Timothy 4:7).

Water of the Word

This past summer we made a trip from Montana to Washington. As we drove west on 90, we left the mountains and entered what was once a "dry and thirsty" land before the Columbia Basin Project. The project now pumps irrigation water to over 671,000 acres in central Washington. The land was always **fertile;** it just needed water to become **fruitful.**

As I stood on a plateau seeing the contrast between irrigated and not irrigated land, I thought how true it is in my life. The water of the Word makes the difference. It is God's desire that I have a fruitful life: *"I am come that they might have life, and that they might have it more abundantly"* (John 10:10).

Not just my life, but the life of every believer. Without the Word of God, we can become barren, unproductive, and subject to destruction. The presence of the Holy Spirit fertilizes our heart, and we need the water of the Word to produce fruit. Our faith grows as a result of the Water of the Word. *"So then faith cometh by hearing, and hearing by the word of God"* (Romans 10:17).

It is also God's desire that we be set apart so He might present us to Himself holy and blameless. This can only be accomplished by our being immersed in the Word:

"That he might sanctify [set apart] *and cleanse* [regenerate] *it* [her- the church] *with the washing of water by the word* [truth], *That he might present it to himself a glorious church, not having spot, or wrinkle, or any such thing; but that it should be holy and without blemish"* (Ephesians 5:26-27).

Bill often says: "If you neglect the Word of God, you will fail. It may not be a huge, catastrophic failure that everyone will see; instead it may be a failure that spells a barely-get-by Christianity."

I don't know about you, but I don't want to live an unproductive, fruitless, "barely get by" Christian life. The solution: **Be irrigated by the water of the Word!**

Enter Into His Rest

*"Let us labour therefore to enter into that rest,
lest any man fall after the same example of unbelief."*
(Hebrews 4:11)

The *rest* spoken of in verse 11 does not have the same meaning as spoken of in verse 4 *"God did rest,"* referring to His resting from creation. Rather it is a forward thrust, challenging us to trust God for what He has done in redeeming us, and daily enjoy all the spiritual blessings as we walk by faith according to the truth of His Word.

"Let us therefore fear, lest, a promise being left us of entering into his rest, any of you should seem to come short of it." (Hebrews 4:1)

The author talks about the fear of *not believing* God. "Not believing" will keep us from entering into the rest God intends for us to enjoy. First, by not believing in the Gospel which leads to salvation. Second, by not believing the truth Jesus spoke, *"I am come that they might have life, and that they might have it more abundantly"* (John 10:10).

"Lest any man fall…" does not refer to the loss of salvation, but rather to lose out on God's provisions for this abundant life through a lack of faith.

"Let us labour…" stresses urgency, attentiveness, a quickness to enter into this rest. The example of unbelief the author is referring to here is the unbelief of the ten spies at Kadesh, the unbelief in the power of God to perform what He had promised.

Only those who believe, hear His voice, and harden not their hearts may enter into His rest. Not as a result of their own work, but as a result of believing and trusting in His power to perform all that He has promised. (Hebrews. 4:6-10)

I challenge you (as I do myself) to look back and evaluate: Have I entered into His rest? Am I trusting in Him, believing His promises, walking daily according to the spiritual blessings found in the Word of God? Am I relying on my own "works" or am I truly resting in His power? The choice is ours.

Leaky Brain

When we were planting our last church in Florida, we drove our children to school an hour away. Our daily commute included three different back roads as well as 15 miles on I-75. On more than one occasion, as we were driving along, I would realize I didn't know where I was on the route—sometimes not even remembering if I had made a turn. Why was that? Well, it was because I wasn't paying attention.

I have forgotten something or neglected to do something simply because I didn't pay attention to the instructions. *"Therefore we ought to give the more earnest heed to the things which we have heard, lest at any time we should let them slip"* (Hebrews 2:1).

'Give' means to attach ourselves to and *'more earnest'* adds an urgency to it. An urgency to pay strict attention to the Word of God, *"lest at any time we should let them slip."* While studying this phrase, I found two different images:

1. When we do not pay attention, the Word does not register and will soon **'drift away.'**

2. When we do not pay attention, the Word can **'leak out'**—go in one ear and out the other.

We should profit from reading the Word of God, because the truth should benefit us. *"All scripture is given by inspiration of God . . . That the man of God may be perfect, thoroughly furnished unto all good works"* (2 Timothy 3:16-17).

My challenge to myself and you is: 1) Recognize that the Word of God is important and valuable for everyday living; 2) Don't allow the busyness and cares of life to claim all of our attention; and 3) Do not neglect the Word because of the pleasures of this life.

"And that which fell among thorns are they, which, when they have heard, go forth, and are choked with cares and riches and pleasures of this life, and bring no fruit to perfection. But that on the good ground are they, which in an honest and good heart, having heard the word, keep it, and bring forth fruit with patience" (Luke 8:14-15).

On To Perfection

"Therefore leaving the principles of the doctrine of Christ, let us go on unto perfection" (Hebrews 6:1). The term *'leaving'* does not mean to separate from, but rather it implies passing from one phase to another.

The writer of Hebrews lists six specific areas from which our *perfection (*spiritual maturity*)* is to come. Repentance from dead works, faith toward God, the doctrine of baptisms, the laying on of hands, the resurrection of the dead and eternal judgement.

"And this we will do, if God permits" (Hebrews 6:3). God fully expects us to mature and develop holiness; however, it is a process impossible to do without God: *"For it is God which worketh in you both to will and to do of his good pleasure"* (Philippians 2:13).

Since there is a possibility of our choosing not to *"go on"*, a warning is given: *"For it is impossible for those who were once enlightened . . . If they shall fall away, to renew them again unto repentance; seeing they crucify to themselves the Son of God afresh, and put him to an open shame"* (Hebrews 6:4-6). Not the lost of salvation- but one can come to the point when the consequences of disobedience cannot be reversed.

I am witnessing this in the life of a friend who has tasted the things of Christ for many years, and now is choosing to deliberately turn her back on the things of Christ. According to God's Word, she could lose the possibility of repentance. Even if she should change her mind, God will forbid her to recover lost opportunities.

By abiding in Christ, we can mature and thus receive the blessings from God: answered prayer, inner satisfaction, the warmth of His love and genuine joy. *"For the earth which drinketh in the rain that cometh oft upon it, and bringeth forth herbs meet for them by whom it is dressed, receiveth blessing from God:"* (Hebrews 6:7)

May the conviction of my heart and yours be to move on to perfection; to be spiritually alert, teachable and sensitive to divine direction.

The Hope of God

"Which **hope** *we have as an anchor of the soul, both sure and steadfast, and which entereth into that within the veil; Whither the forerunner is for us entered, even Jesus, made an high priest for ever after the order of Melchisedec"* (Hebrews 6:19,20).

Hope refers to the oath given by God, *"In hope of eternal life, which God, that cannot lie, promised before the world began"* (Titus 1:2).

At times, our life can be hard, storms can toss us about; but be encouraged - we have a hope that serves as an anchor for life itself. The function of an anchor is to keep the ship from moving from its position. The anchor cannot be seen, yet it can be depended upon to keep the ship from drifting. *"Therefore we ought to give the more earnest heed to the things which we have heard, lest at any time we should let them slip [drift away]"* (Hebrews 2:1).

Our hope of eternal fellowship with God should keep us from drifting away especially when the winds blow and the waves seem to overtake us.

This hope is *sure* - indestructible; nothing can *"separate us from the love of God"* (Romans 8:35-39). This hope is *stedfast* - no weakness can be found in it. This hope is found in the very presence of God. This hope is Jesus! He has gone before us and has promised to return to take us to glory. *"And if I go and prepare a place for you, I will come again, and receive you unto myself; that where I am, there ye may be also"* (John 14:3).

♫ We have an anchor that keeps the soul, steadfast and sure while the billows roll, fastened to the Rock which cannot move. Grounded firm and deep in the Savior's Love. ♫

May we bear trials patiently and without complaint in the hope of our future glory, the blessed eternity with our Lord.

"But if we hope for that we see not, then do we with patience wait for it" (Rom 8:25).

New Covenant

Several years ago, after reading through the Old Testament about the sacrifices needed to be made on a regular basis for sins to be forgiven and in order to receive the blessings of God, a new believer expressed her happiness over the fact that she did <u>not</u> have to "do those things".

I was reminded of her comment while studying through the book of Hebrews. *"But now hath he (Jesus Christ) obtained a more excellent ministry, by how much also he is the mediator of a better covenant, which was established upon better promises"* (Hebrews 8:6).

The earthly priests were imperfect and their ministry was based on ceremony, but Jesus' ministry is more excellent because it is perfect, effective and continuous.

*He is the mediator (*not a middleman, but the guarantee*) of a better covenant* - the old covenant was based on man's obedience but the new covenant is based upon the sacrifice of Jesus Christ, God's faithfulness (not ours) and the truth of God's Word.

- established upon better promises - the old covenant depended upon the promises man made toward God; what man could do for God. *"Now therefore, if ye will obey my voice indeed, and keep my covenant, . .And all the people answered together, and said, All that the Lord hath spoken we will do"* (Exodus 19:5, 8). The new covenant focuses on God's promises of what He will do within man.

We have received a *better covenant.* A covenant based upon God's determined purpose to change us from the inside out; to produce an eternal living relationship between us and Himself. *"I will put my laws into their mind, and write them in their hearts: and I will be to them a God, and they shall be to me a people"* (Hebrews 8:10).

May we recognized the wonderful truth of the new covenant given to us and live accordingly.

"This is a faithful saying, and these things I will that thou affirm constantly, that they which have believed in God might be careful to maintain good works. These things are good and profitable unto men" (Titus 3:8).

Time for a Decision

In Hebrews when the writer's argument for the superiority of Jesus Christ is basically over, he begins to focus on the practical application.

"Let us <u>draw near</u> with a true heart in full assurance of faith having our hearts sprinkled from an evil conscience and our bodies washed with pure water"(Hebrews 10:22).

We must come to God fully persuaded of and confidence in God's power and promises Because of Christ's sacrifice, our hearts have been made clean and we can walk boldly into the presence of God.

"Let us <u>hold fast</u> the profession of our faith without wavering; (for he is faithful that promised)" (Hebrews 10:23).

Genuine salvation is faith in the deity of Christ, His death, burial, and resurrection. As believers we can commit our trust to God whose faithfulness is beyond questioning.

"And let us <u>consider</u> one another to provoke unto love and to good works: Not forsaking the assembling of ourselves together, as the manner of some is; but exhorting one another: and so much the more, as ye see the day approaching." (Hebrews 10:24, 25).

The word 'consider' implies thoughtful perception and serious concern. God actually wants us to put some effort into provoking one another *unto love and to good works*. Too many times, we think of provoke in terms of a negative action (irritating, annoying, maddening). Here it is a positive action; to provoke in order to sharpen and encourage growth: "*Iron sharpeneth iron; so a man sharpeneth the countenance of his friend*" (Proverbs 27:17). Unity and strength comes from working together while division only creates weakness.

The Bible teaches that each member of the body needs the other members.

My challenge is to take thoughtful and serious consideration to be a part of a local church and to take advantage of every opportunity to fellowship with believers. You need it and so do they!

Faith and Obedience

"Wherefore seeing we also are compassed about with so great a cloud of witnesses, let us lay aside every weight, and the sin which doth so easily beset us, and let us run with patience the race that is set before us" (Hebrews 12:1).

Reading this verse brought to mind something our son, Clint, wrote regarding his twin brother, Cliff:

"Attending Clifford's memorial was a real eye-opener for me. For the first time I saw my brother through other people. I got a glimpse of him as a colleague, a teacher, a son, a husband, in ways I hadn't really seen before. I saw how much his cancer had changed him in ways I hadn't understood. I saw the impact that a man could have when he really knew God—when he really cultivated a dependency on the Lord. And I had the same thought that he would have had in my place: if he can do it, then so can I!"

The cloud of witnesses is a representation of those listed in chapter 11 who have themselves been in the same race, and their witness to us testifies of God's faithfulness. They did not simply believe the truth of God but acted out in obedience to the truth of God. They show us it is possible to live by faith, and we ought to act as if they were cheering us on.

"But wilt thou know, O vain man, that faith without works is dead." (James 2:20) *"For as the body without the spirit is dead, so faith without works is dead also."* (James 2:26)

James and the writer of Hebrews are saying the same thing: **Faith and obedience MUST accompany each other**.

The list of heroes is meant to provide the readers (you and me) with encouragement as we face our own difficult circumstances; that we might see *the impact that a man could have when he really knew God – when he really cultivated a dependency on the Lord.*

Our response needs to be: **If they can do it, then so can we!**

A Good Conscience

As I came to the end of my study through Hebrews, I was challenged by the author's request for prayer that he would maintain certain qualities of spiritual integrity and leadership.

"Pray for us: for we trust we have a good conscience, in all things willing to live honestly (Hebrews 13:18). Paul refers to a good conscience as being *void of any offence toward God, and toward men"* (Acts 24:16).

Before salvation, distinguishing between what is morally good and bad is pretty much ruled by our environment and/or the way we were raised. Over 21 years ago during a stopover in Rome, a group of us decided to take a tour bus to see the sights. While waiting for the bus, we saw mothers openly nursing their babies for the sole purpose of distracting the "tourists" so their young children could pick pockets. This may shock us, but to them, their actions bring no guilt or shame; it is simply a way to provide for the family.

When we accept Christ as our Savior, the Holy Spirit causes our moral compass to be recalibrated. What is morally good and bad now has a true north. A good conscience is not a once for all event; it is a daily cleansing. *"Search me, O God, and know my heart: try me, and know my thought"* (Psalms 139:23). Left unchecked, sin can "sear" our conscience; *"speaking lies in hypocrisy; having their conscience seared with a hot iron"* (1 Timothy 4:2).

The author goes on in vs 20 to identify God as *"the God of Peace".* The ultimate result of a good conscience is peace: *"And let the peace of God rule in your hearts"* (Colossians 3:15).

"But glory, honour, and peace, to every man that worketh good" (Romans 2:10).

"And as many as walk according to this rule, peace be on them" (Galatians 6:16).

My challenge is that you and I would be able to say; *"Men and brethren, I have lived in all good conscience before God until this day"* (Acts 23:1).

Abundant Life

"I am come that they might have life, and that they might have it more abundantly" (John 10:10).

Life more abundantly does not mean we will not hurt physically or emotionally. So what does having an abundant life mean?

The context of John 10:10 is Jesus Christ as the great Shepherd. Therefore we have **Confidence in the Shepherd's care**: *"The Lord is my shepherd; I shall not want. He maketh me to lie down in green pastures: he leadeth me beside the still waters. He restoreth my soul: he leadeth me in the paths of righteousness for his name's sake"* (Psalms 23 1-5).

We can experience **Personal peace and joy**: *"Peace I leave with you, my peace I give unto you: not as the world giveth, give I unto you. Let not your heart be troubled, neither let it be afraid"* (John 14:27).

We do have a responsibility, and that is to separate ourselves from sin and commit ourselves to righteousness to live the abundant life. Be **Partakers of God's Holiness**: *"Submit yourselves therefore to God. Resist the devil, and he will flee from you. Draw nigh to God, and he will draw nigh to you. Cleanse your hands, ye sinners; and purify your hearts, ye double minded. . .Humble yourselves in the sight of the Lord, and he shall lift you up"* (James 4:7-10).

Finally understand that we have been **Sanctified for His use**: *"And now, brethren, I commend you to God, and to the word of his grace, which is able to build you up, and to give you an inheritance among all them which are sanctified"* (Acts 20:32).

Go forth and enjoy this abundant life in Jesus Christ being confident that *"According as his divine power hath given unto us all things that pertain unto life and godliness, through the knowledge of him that hath called us to glory and virtue: Whereby are given unto us exceeding great and precious promises: that by these ye might be partakers of the divine nature, having escaped the corruption that is in the world through lust"* (2 Peter 1:3-4).

Is There Any Word from the Lord?

"But, beloved, be not ignorant of this one thing, that one day is with the Lord as a thousand years, and a thousand years as one day" (2 Peter 3:8).

The Old Testament records God setting the Jewish people apart as His chosen nation, the rise and fall of kings and rulers, battles and captivities, the rebuilding of the temple and rebuilding the wall around Jerusalem. Between the Old Testament and New, there are four hundred years of silence when there was no direct communication from God. Yet God was continuing to prepare the world for the coming of Jesus Christ.

I did some research to find out what happened in those four hundred years. It was during those years that some of Daniel's prophecies were fulfilled. The Greek culture spread making Greek the common language in which the New Testament would eventually be written. The Hebrew Old Testament was translated into the Greek language. It was this translation that was used in the synagogues and was read by the early churches. The Jews became tired of oppression; they developed a longing for a military and political messiah. Antioch grew and would eventually become the first major outreach of the Gospel and Paul's home church. Two religious political powers emerged: forerunners of the Pharisees and the Sadducees. The priests had power among the Jewish people and Roman rule created unrest. It was into this world that Jesus came.

There are times in our life when we think God is silent, yet He is preparing us for a specific task or event in our life. *"For it is God which worketh in you both to will and to do of his good pleasure"* (Philippians 2:13).

As His children (John 1:12), we can go forward with confidence! The Word of God and the indwelling of the Holy Spirit assures each believer that God IS at work in their life. *"In whom also we have obtained an inheritance, being predestinated according to the purpose of him who worketh all things after the counsel of his own will"* (Ephesians 1:11).

Freedom

"And ye shall know the truth, and the truth shall make you free" (John 8:3).

Free from the curse of sin: *"But now being made free from sin, and become servants to God"* (Romans 6:22).

Free from the bondage that sorrow, misfortune, affliction, heartache, discouragement, and tragedy can bring: *"Stand fast therefore in the liberty wherewith Christ hath made us free, and be not entangled again with the yoke of bondage"* (Galatians. 5:1). Paul instructs us to *"stand fast."* When sin comes knocking at our door, we do not have to open it. Christ has provided the means in which we can have freedom.

Free to have hope and joy in the daily struggles of life. This spring, when visiting my daughter in Alaska, I woke up with stiffness in my neck which created severe pain in my shoulder blade and down my arm. When I arrived back home, I began treatment but it was limited because of our leaving for Montana. I was given a referral and began seeing a chiropractor in Anaconda. Now, I am home and the bills are arriving. What I thought was covered by insurance is not because I did not get approval for out of network medical care. The expenses include x-rays and an MRI. Although caused by my own human error, I rest in: *"And we know that all things work together for good to them that love God, to them who are the called according to his purpose"* (Romans 8:28).

At salvation, I was set free from the penalty of sin. Now I must live truth to experience freedom from the stress and anxiety which are knocking at my door. *"Be careful for nothing; but in everything by prayer and supplication with thanksgiving let your requests be made known unto God and the peace of God, which passeth all understanding, shall keep your hearts and minds through Christ Jesus"* (Philippians. 4:6-7). *"Casting all your care upon him; for he careth for you"* (1 Peter 5:7).

What in your life today would take you captive? **Stand fast – in Christ you have been set free!**

Holy Spirit

"Howbeit when he, the Spirit of truth, is come, he will guide you into all truth: for he shall not speak of himself; but whatsoever he shall hear, that shall he speak: and he will shew you things to come. He shall glorify me: for he shall receive of mine, and shall shew it unto you" (John 16:13-14).

"Whereby are given unto us exceeding great and precious promises: that by these ye might be partakers of the divine nature . . ." (2 Peter 1:4).

Of all the promises given in the New Testament, The Holy Spirit is the greatest. God Himself coming to dwell in us. The very same Holy Spirit who breathed the very Words of God into the hearts of the men chosen to record them is the same Spirit who activates His Word in our hearts and minds.

When we claim the verse I can do all things through Christ who strengthens me, we are claiming the power of Christ in us; the Holy Spirit. The Bible tells us the Holy Spirit automatically takes up residence in every believer at the time of salvation, but it commands us to be filled with the Holy Spirit; then we can conquer temptation, bear unbearable pains, love and forgive, and accomplished the work He has called to do.

"See, I have set before thee this day life and good, and death and evil" (Deuteronomy 30:15). I recently read that the difference between these two choices is the spirit of Satan will never be able to unite himself with our spirit, where, on the other hand, the Spirit of God unites Himself full with us that we become the temple of the Holy Spirit. Yes, Jesus Christ has fully conquered this battle. But as always, the choice is up to us. *"Neither yield ye your members as instruments of unrighteousness unto sin: but yield yourselves unto God"* (Romans 6:14).

My challenge: Give thanks for the indwelling Holy Spirit for He will teach us, guide us and enable us to do the work of Him who saved us.

Why is it a Merry Christmas?

For who He is: *"For in him dwelleth all the fullness of the Godhead bodily"* (Colossians. 2:9).

John refers to Jesus Christ as:

The WORD. The Word expresses all that God has revealed or shall reveal of Himself to the world. *"In the beginning was the Word, and the Word was with God, and the Word was God. . .and the Word became flesh and dwelt among us, and we beheld His glory"* (John 1:14).

The LIFE. *"In Him was life; and the life was the light of men"* (John 1:4). Life lived by God, lived humanly among us – *"For as the Father hath life in himself; so hath he given to the Son to have life in himself"* (John 5:26). And life that is given to all who trust Christ as their Savior: *"He that hath the son hath life; he that hath not the Son of God hath not the life"* (1 John 5:12).

The LIGHT. *"That* [referring to Jesus] *was the true light, which lighteth every man that cometh into the world"* (John 1:9). The Light is pure truth, pure holiness, and pure blessedness. As the Light of men, He is the source and giver of knowledge, righteousness, and life—*"Then spake Jesus again unto them, saying, 'I am the light of the world: he that followeth me shall not walk in darkness, but shall have the light of life'"* (John 8:12). *"I am come a light into the world, that whosoever believeth on me should not abide in darkness"* (John 12:46).

As believers in Jesus Christ who is **the WORD, the LIFE, and the LIGHT**, we should not walk in ignorance, sin, or hopelessness. Believing in the Incarnate Christ, we can look forward to that day when we shall see Him face to face. *"And they shall see his face; and his name shall be in their foreheads. And there shall be no night there; and they need no candle, neither light of the sun; for the Lord God giveth them light: and they shall reign for ever and ever"* (Revelations 22:4-5).

Do ALL to the Glory of God

"Whether you eat or drink or whatever you do, do it all for the Glory of God" (1 Corinthians 10:31).

Throughout these past several years, I determined to get to know Jesus Christ better through His Word. I have come to realize that God's expectations of me are actually privileges I have because of my relationship with HIM. Yes, it is a privilege: *"For ye are bought with a price: therefore <u>glorify God</u> in your body, and in your spirit, which are God's"* (1 Corinthinans 6:20). *"Thou art worthy, O Lord, to receive glory and honor and power: for thou hast created all things, and for thy pleasure they are and were created"* (Revelations 4:11).

By definition we are to bestow honor, praise, or admiration; to light up brilliantly or to represent as glorious. We are to bring to light His Glory, to represent Him in our lives so others might be drawn to Him. 1 Corinthians 10:31 was written in regard to our liberty; whether our choices offend a brother or are a stumbling block to the unbeliever. *"Let your light so shine before men, that they may see your good works, and glorify your Father which is in heaven"* (Matthew 5:16).

"These words spoke Jesus, and lifted up his eyes to heaven, and said, Father, the hour is come; glorify thy Son, that thy Son also may glorify thee: As thou hast given him power over all flesh, that he should give eternal life to as many as thou hast given him. And this is life eternal, that they might know thee the only true God, and Jesus Christ, whom thou hast sent. I have glorified thee on the earth: I have finished the work which thou gavest me to do" (John 17:1-5).

My goal based upon Scripture, is to approach everything in light of God and eternity so I may one day say: I have glorified you on earth: I have finished the work you gave me to do.

I challenge you as I challenge myself; if it cannot be done to the glory of God – Don't do it!

Christian Liberty

"Wherefore receive ye one another, as Christ also received us to the Glory of God" (Romans 15:7).

Paul spends some time giving guidelines in the area of Christian Liberty. Ultimately, a believer's responsibility is to God; yet everything they do affects someone else. One's liberties should be used for the edification of others, not for their own pleasure. Nor should they be a stumbling block (attitude or action that causes another believer to sin or to become confused about God's character and purposes) and weaken another believer's spiritual condition. See: Romans 14:13-15:3.

Freedom in Christ should never be characterized by criticism, ridicule or judgment of others. Rather is should be characterized by love; focusing on the needs of others and fostering a spirit of harmony among God's people. There is no place for selfishness.

Christian Liberty can be accompanied with the attitude "I am more spiritual than you, so I can do it" or "I am so spiritual, I don't do it". Spirituality does not come from following a list of do's or don'ts but rather a life yielded to the Holy Spirit.

Of course, we don't have the same problem Paul addresses in Romans regarding eating meat from idols, but there are Christians who are passionate about their "rights". Regardless of what that "right" is, the principle of righteousness is always in affect. Is it in violation of God's Word? Will it bring us further along in our walk with Christ? Will it cause a sister in Christ to stumble? Will it hinder another from being saved? Will it bring glory to God? We are ultimately responsible to God, and will give account for our actions at the judgement seat of Christ; *"for we shall all stand before the judgment seat of Christ . . .So then everyone of us shall give account of himself to God* " (Romans 14:10,12).

"Now may the God of patience and comfort grant you to be likeminded toward one another, according to Christ Jesus, that you may with one mind and one mouth glorify the God and father of our Lord Jesus Christ" (Romans 15:5).

Perfect Love

The source of this love - God:
- *"In this was manifested the love of God toward us, because that God sent his only begotten Son into the world. . ."* (1 John 4:9).
- *"But God, who is rich in mercy, for his great love wherewith he loved us. Even when we were dead in sins, hath quickened us together with Christ"* (Ephesians 2:4-5).
There is nothing we can do, think or say that will cause Him to love us more, and nothing that will cause Him to love us less.

The model of this love - Christ:
- *"But God commendeth his love toward us, in that, while we were yet sinners, Christ died for us"* (Romans 5:8).
Not only did Christ model this love through his death, but also through His submission to God the Father while he walked here on earth: the laying aside of His Godly robe and being born as a babe in a lowly stable, enduring the fierce attacks of Satan in the wilderness, facing ridicule and betrayer and finally the horrible beatings before his crucifixion.

The extent of this love – sacrifice of life:
- *"For God so loved the world, that he gave his only begotten Son"* (John 3:16).

The results of this love – abiding presence of God:
- *"God is love; and he that dwelleth in love dwelleth in God, and God in him"* (1 John 4:16).

The goal of this love - to have us with Him throughout eternity:
- *". . . that we might live through him"* (1 John 4:9).
- *". . . that whosoever believeth in him should not perish, but have everlasting life"* (John 3:16).

The challenge is to manifest this love to others. It doesn't come naturally, but through the ministry of the Holy Spirit, it can be a reality in our lives.
- *"Beloved, if God so loved us, we ought also to love one another. No man hath seen God at any time. If we love one another, God dwelleth in us, and his love is perfected in us"* (1 John 4:11-12).
- *". . .Thou shalt love thy neighbour as thyself"* (Matthew 22:39).

The Loving Kindness of God

As we pass another anniversary of our son's entrance into heaven, my mind replays those last two weeks. *"Oh that men would praise the LORD for his goodness and for his wonderful works to the children of men"* (Psalms 107:15).

I had gone to enjoy a week with him and Megan: Perhaps we would go to Rhode Island to mark it off my "states visited" list. He would be starting chemo and I was happy to be able to take him to get his port put in. God's plan overrode ours. He wonderfully and gloriously allowed me to be there for Cliff's last days.

Yes, I replay those days in my mind: The moment in the ER when he said; "mom, we always knew this day would come." My response; "yes, but we always thought it would be in the future." He wisely said; "mom, this is the future." At one point he asked me how I was doing. I responded; "not so well, you are going to heaven, and I have to stay here." He never asked again. He would simply say: "I love you, Mom." Those words still resound in my ears! I have the memory of holding his hand as I sat quietly by his side, and the words I spoke as he stepped over the threshold of Heaven seeing Jesus face to face. These memories are a glorious reminder of God's kindness to me!

Someone likened death as taking down the tent and journeying on to another world. Cliff prepared for it by investing in the lives of his students; by continually reminding them of the goodness of God and his loving kindness to his children. *"For the LORD God is a sun and shield: the LORD will give grace and glory: no good thing will he withhold from them that walk uprightly"* (Psalms 84:11). His life reflected all he taught.

What does our life reflect as we prepare for the journey? *"Seeing then that all these things shall be dissolved, what manner of persons ought ye to be in all holy conversation and godliness"* (2 Peter 3:11).

A Servant and a Slave

"Simon Peter, a servant and an apostle of Jesus Christ ,to them that have obtained like precious faith with us through the righteousness of God and our Savior Jesus Christ" (2 Peter 1:1).

Those who have received Jesus Christ as their Savior are in the position of being a slave; *"Ye are bought with a price"* (1 Corinthians 6:20). I was reminded as I began a study of 2 Peter that this position should not be taken lightly. To be a slave of God means to be possessed by God; not should be or could be, but ARE. As the master, He has the power over us; the power of life or death. As His slave, we are at the disposal of God without question; constantly in His service.   We cannot tell God when or where we want to serve: "I will, but . . .", or "I won't". I tried that once, it did not work! We are to be like the servant in Deuteronomy 15:16-17 who loved his master and was quite satisfied to serve his master.

With the privilege of being a servant of a living God comes a great responsibility and accountability. *"For we must all appear before the judgement seat of Christ; that every one may receive the things done in his body, according to that he hath done, whether it be good or bad"* (2 Corinthians 5:10).

A servant is three things: obedient, dependable and accountable. REJOICE! God enables us to be obedient, dependable and accountable. *"Grace and Peace be multiplied unto you through the knowledge of God, and of Jesus our Lord"* (2 Peter 1:1, 2). Another one of those co-ops!

Peter declares himself first a servant and then an Apostle (sent one). One should automatically follow the other. *"Ye have not chosen me, but I have chosen you, and ordained you, that Ye should go and bring forth fruit, and that your fruit should remain"* (John 15:16).

"Make me a servant, humble and weak, Lord, let me lift up those who are weak, and may the prayer of my heart always be: Make me a servant today."

Divine Balance

"According as to His Divine Power hath given us all things that pertain to life and godliness through the knowledge of Him who has called us to glory and virtue. Whereby are given unto us exceedingly great and precious promises that by these we might be partakers of the divine nature having escaped the corruption that is in the world through lust" (2 Peter 1:3,4).

There is a balance of human and divine cooperation in accomplishing God's purpose. Some may say it doesn't matter what we do, if God wants it done, it will be done. Others have the mindset that it is up to us to get it done. God will not do for us what we can do ourselves, but God will do for us what we cannot do for ourselves.

God has given us:
Faith - without it, we cannot please Him.
Grace - enables us to trust, to respond as Christ would respond, to give and to serve.
Peace - because of Grace, we can have an inward rest and wellbeing.
Great & Precious Promises - some things can be great, but not valuable; some things can be valuable, but not great. God's Promises are both!
Divine Nature – not only at the beginning of our Spiritual journey but those attributes reflected in His children's walk - love, mercy, compassion and holiness.

In light of all God has given us: we have a responsibility. *"And beside this giving all diligence, add to your faith . . ."* (2 Peter 1:5). Peter says to give careful and persistent work to add to our faith. It comes down to (once again) us making a choice.

We must appropriate His promises (John 1:12), we must recognize we are in Christ and Christ is in us (Ephesians 2:6), we must allow the Holy Spirit to work in our lives (Galatians 5:16), we must submit to Him and worship Him

"O, come let us worship and bow down: let us kneel before the Lord our maker. For He is our God; and we are his people, the sheep of His hand" (Psalms 95:6, 7).

Spiritual Advance

God expects us to advance in our Christian walk. If we are not advancing then we are retreating; there is no standing still.

"And besides this, giving all diligence: Add to your faith virtue; and to virtue knowledge; and to knowledge temperance; and to temperance patience; and to patience godliness; and to godliness brotherly kindness; and to brotherly kindness charity" (2 Peter 1:5-7).

We are to add to the foundation of faith **virtue**: excellence; not only striving for spiritual excellence, but fulfilling our purpose in life by glorifying god because we have God's nature within us. It is not improving human qualities, but producing divine qualities that make us more like Jesus Christ.

To virtue **knowledge**: a common sense. Knowledge gives us the wisdom to act in a God honoring way as we encounter day to day circumstances and decisions.

To knowledge **temperance**: self-control. *"He that hath no rule over his own spirit is like a city that is broken down and without walls"* (Proverbs 25:28).
"Exercise thyself rather unto godliness" (1 Timothy 2:7).

To temperance **patience**: endurance and steadfastness. Bill calls this a conquering endurance; handling the pressures and problems of life with courage and confidence.

To patience **godliness**: God-likeness. It speaks of a conscience awareness of God in every aspect of life. Godliness is seeking to do God's will as well as looking out for the welfare of others.

To godliness **brotherly kindness**: *"If a man say, I love God, but hates his brother, he is a liar: for he that Loves not his brother whom he hath seen, how can he love God whom he hath not seen"* (1 John 4:20).

To brotherly kindness **charity**: Agape love. *"Hereby perceive we the love of God, because he laid down his life for us: and we ought to lay down our lives for the brethren"* (1 John 3:16).

It is through the power of God and the promises of God that this growth takes place --2 Peter 1:3, 4. Knowing this, may we diligently advance in our spiritual walk appropriating all that He has given us?

Win or Lose

It should be a common thing for a believer to be fruitful. God has given us *"all things that pertain to life and godliness" and "great and precious promises"*. We are to *"give all diligence"* adding to our faith virtue, knowledge, temperance, patience, godliness, brotherly kindness and charity (2 Peter 1:3-7). If you have these you win; if not, you lose.

*"For if these things be in you and abound, they make you that **ye shall neither be barren nor unfruitful** in the knowledge of our Lord Jesus Christ"* (2 Peter 1:8).

You **win** the assurance of fruitfulness: you WILL BE useful and fruitful. It is interesting that the verse says "in you and abound". It isn't how busy you are, it is what is inside of you: It is who you are - not what you do. This fruitfulness is centered around knowledge of the Word of God producing an intimate relationship with Christ demonstrating the fruit of the Spirit: *"love, joy, peace, longsuffering, gentleness, goodness, faithfulness, meekness, and temperance"* (Galatians. 5:22,23), and a life that wins souls; *"The fruit of the righteous is a tree of life; and he that winners souls is wise"* (Proverbs 11:30).

*"But he that lacketh these thing **is blind** and **cannot see afar off** and **hath forgotten** that he was purged of his old sins"* (2 Peter 1:9).

You **lose** the ability to see what He wants you to see. Your eyes are so fixed on the here and now; you cannot focus on the eternal truths. The reality of your salvation dims even to the point of questioning it: a spiritual blindness.

Peter encouraged believers to *"give diligence to make your calling and election sure for if ye do these things, ye will never fail: for so an entrance shall be ministered unto you abundantly into the everlasting kingdom of our Lord and Savior Jesus Christ"* (2 Peter 1:10-11).

Be diligent in living out who we are in Christ; for we will receive the greatest reward- the victor's entrance into the everlasting kingdom!

Eyewitness

"For we have not followed cunningly devised fables. . . But were eyewitnesses of his majesty. For he received from God the Father honor and glory" (2 Peter 1:16, 17).

Peter had the privilege of seeing and hearing Jesus receive honor and glory from His Father in Heaven. Peter was an eye witness to the majesty of Jesus Christ.

This phase - *eye witness to his majesty* - stuck with me. I may not have been an eye witness to the Transfiguration, but I do have the privilege to be an eye witness to majesty of Christ in my life.

"For it is the power of God unto salvation" (Romans 1:16). I was an eyewitness to the power of salvation when at the age of 19, the Holy Spirit convicted my heart and I asked Jesus Christ to forgive my sins and come into my heart.

I am an eye witness to God's power in changing my life from who I was to who I am now. *"I am crucified with Christ: nevertheless I live; yet not I, but Christ liveth in me: and the life I now live in the flesh I live by the faith of the Son of God, who loved me, and gave himself for me"* (Galatians 2:20).

I witness His Majesty through the Word of God, and I look forward to one day seeing Him in all of His Glory. *"We have also a more sure word of prophecy. . .as unto a light that shineth in a dark place, until the day dawn, and the day star arise in your hearts"* (2 Peter 1:19).

God has given us the truth; NOT man's thoughts and ideas. *"no prophecy of the scripture is of any private interpretation. For the prophecy came not in old time by the will of man; but holy men of God spake as they were by the Holy Ghost"* (2 Peter 1:20-21).

Are you an eye-witness? Be faithful in sharing Christ in all of His Majesty.
"For we cannot but speak the things which we have seen and heard" (Acts 4:20).

God Has the Final Say

In 2 Peter 1, Peter reminds us of our resources in Christ: faith, grace, peace, power, and precious promises. He reminds us that the Word of God is never failing and is divinely inspired.   Peter then turns his attention to false teachers who undermines the power and authority of God's Word.

Believers are warned not to be taken in by false doctrine and the deception of false teachers. There were false prophets in the Old Testament, there were false teacher during Peter's time and today there continues to be those who would twist God's Word and those who out and out deny the Truth ". . . *the way of the truth shall be evil spoken of"* (2 Peter 2:2).

Christianity is being challenged, and the rights of believers in Jesus Christ are in danger. Three examples from the Old Testament are given to encourage us. *"The Lord knoweth how to deliver the godly* [Noah & Lot] *out of temptations, and to reserve the unjust* [angels] *unto the day of judgement to be punished"* (2 Peter 2:9). God judgement is sure and the day of reckoning for the ungodly is coming.

Peter goes on to *"stir up your pure minds by way of remembrance"* (2 Peter 3:1). There will be scoffer and those who question the truth of God's Word regarding the coming of the Lord. But as my husband, Bill, would say; "to God timing is more important than time." **God will keep His promise** and what is perceived as a delay to us is due to the longsuffering of God: *"not willing that any should perish, but that all should come to repentance"* (2 Peter 3:8).

God uses Peter to convey a challenge to those who have trusted in Christ as their Savior:
 "what manner of persons ought ye to be in all holy conversation and godliness" (2 Peter 3:11)
 "B*e diligent that ye may be found of him in peace, without spot, and blameless"* (2 Peter 3:14).
"grow in grace, and in the knowledge of our Lord and Savior Jesus Christ" (2 Peter 3:18).

Made in the USA
Middletown, DE
22 March 2019